Charles Lindbergh
Amelia Earhart

Pendulum Press, Inc.
West Haven, Connecticut

COPYRIGHT © 1979 BY PENDULUM PRESS, INC.
All Rights Reserved

ISBN 0-88301-424-6 Complete Set
   0-88301-349-5 Paperback
   0-88301-361-4 Hardcover

Library of Congress Catalog Card Number 79-83614

Published by
Pendulum Press, Inc.
An Academic Industries, Inc. Company
The Academic Building
Saw Mill Road
West Haven, Connecticut 06516

Printed in the United States of America

Charles Lindbergh

Written by
JOHN NORWOOD FAGO

Illustrated by
VICATAN

a
VINCENT FAGO
production

Contents

The Minnesota farm	5-11
Lindbergh's first airplanes	12-17
New York to Paris	18-25
Flying around the world	26-29
Questions for review	30-33

Charles Lindbergh

Charles Augustus Lindbergh was a pioneer* of the air. He was the first man to fly nonstop across the Atlantic Ocean. He took off from New York at dawn on May 20, 1927, and landed in Paris thirty-three and one-half hours later.

The people called him "Lucky Lindy" and "The Lone Eagle" when he returned to New York City. Millions of people turned out to welcome him. He was hardly more than a boy, but his daring solo** flight made him a world hero.

*a person who goes before others, preparing the way for them
**something done alone

6 PENDULUM ILLUSTRATED BIOGRAPHY SERIES

Lindbergh was born in Detroit on February 4, 1902. He was the son of Charles Augustus Lindbergh and Eva Land.

But he grew up in Little Falls, Minnesota, where Pike Creek flows into the Mississippi River.

He lived there with his mother for most of the year.

Thank you for bringing in the wood, Charles.

Each winter Charles and his mother went to Washington, D.C. There they stayed with Charles Lindbergh, Sr. who was a congressman* from Minnesota. Sometimes he took Charles Jr. with him to visit Congress.**

*a person who serves in the U.S. House of Representatives
**a formal meeting of one or both houses of the U.S. government

*a medium-sized bird that comes out only at night

*a narrow step at the side of an automobile on which a person could stand

Charles Lindbergh 9

*try to convince people to vote for someone
**a voting process in which people choose their town, state, and national leaders

Two years later, in the summer of 1915, Congressman Lindbergh was asked to make a trip to the headwaters* of the Mississippi River.

The trip was an important one for young Charles. For six weeks he and his father traveled in wild country. They hunted and fished for their food.

*the source of a river or stream
**a character from a novel who was stranded on a desert island

Charles Lindbergh 11

The next summer Charles' father ran for the Senate, the other house of the U.S. government. Charles drove him around the state to make speeches.

*a tribe of Indians who lived between western Lake Erie and North Dakota
**places where men lived while cutting down trees to make logs

Charles Lindbergh 13

That spring, Charles' parents decided not to live together anymore. The First World War was coming, and Charles' father began making plans for the future.*

You'll be the man in the family now. It may be hard to get food because of the war. I think you'd better run the farm and raise what you need.

Yes, sir.

The farm became Charles' life. At sixteen he was a good farmer who was up every day before dawn.

*But at night he lay in bed and read adventure stories about the pilots in the English** Air Force. He had some dreams of his own.*

*the time to come
**from England

He planned to join the Army Air Corps* as soon as he was old enough. But the war ended, and his mother wanted him to do something else.

Now that the war is over, you can go to college.

But at college, Charles spent more time riding his motorcycle than studying.

You'd be in trouble if your brakes failed going down this hill.

I'll bet I can make the turn at the bottom without using brakes.

The young daredevil** gave it a try.

Luckily, no bones were broken.

You know ... I could do it if I gun the motor just as I make the turn.

*a unit of the army that trained pilots
**someone who tries something very dangerous

Charles Lindbergh 17

On April 26, 1926, Lindbergh flew the first air mail plane between St. Louis and Chicago.

Good work, Slim. You made it in only four hours.

That summer most of his trips were made on time. But when fall came, so did bad weather.

Once he had to parachute* when he could not find a place to land.

But with the help of a friendly farmer and his truck he took his mail bag quickly to a train.

Thanks for the ride!

Good luck, Slim.

*jump from a plane using an umbrella-shaped cloth to break one's fall

PENDULUM ILLUSTRATED BIOGRAPHY SERIES

These were exciting years for Charles. But he had bigger dreams.

Suppose I had a plane with special tanks for extra gasoline...

I could fly all night. I could even fly from New York to Paris.

Then Lindbergh learned that a prize was being offered for this very thing. The first person to fly nonstop from New York to Paris would win $25,000. But he needed help to make the trip. He asked some businessmen for money to buy a plane.

You all love this city, St. Louis. Why not help me buy a plane? We'll call it *The Spirit of St. Louis*. If I make the trip, the name of the city you love will be on the lips of everyone in the world.

It worked. Soon he had enough money.

*a long strip of pavement for airplanes to take off and land

Charles Lindbergh 21

For days, clouds and rain kept everyone on the ground.

Well, if I can't take off, nobody else can, either.

Then reports arrived that the weather over the ocean was clearing.

Good news! I'll go at dawn.

When dawn came, the sky was still cloudy. But Lindbergh, who had always brought the mail through, was ready to go.

I guess the other flyers are waiting for a sunny day to cross the Atlantic.

They can wait as long as they wish, but I want to be first. I'm going!

22 PENDULUM ILLUSTRATED BIOGRAPHY SERIES

The great moment had come. Loaded with 400 gallons of gasoline, the plane started down the runway.

It barely cleared the telephone wires and trees at the end of the runway. But at 7:54 AM on May 20, 1927, The Spirit of St. Louis was on its way to Paris.

To keep his plane light, Lindbergh took no radio. He would find his way by a compass* and by the stars.

*a small instrument which shows direction

Charles Lindbergh 23

That day he flew very low. Often he could see dolphins* leaping over the waves.

As he went north, he flew over a cold ocean filled with icebergs.**

That night the moon rose, and he flew through clouds that seemed like lovely mountains.

He grew tired. Again and again he caught himself falling asleep. He knew that if he slept, the plane would fall into the ocean.

*sea animals usually friendly to man
**large floating masses of ice

*the place where the cliffs of Ireland first rise out of the sea
**a very tall structure in Paris

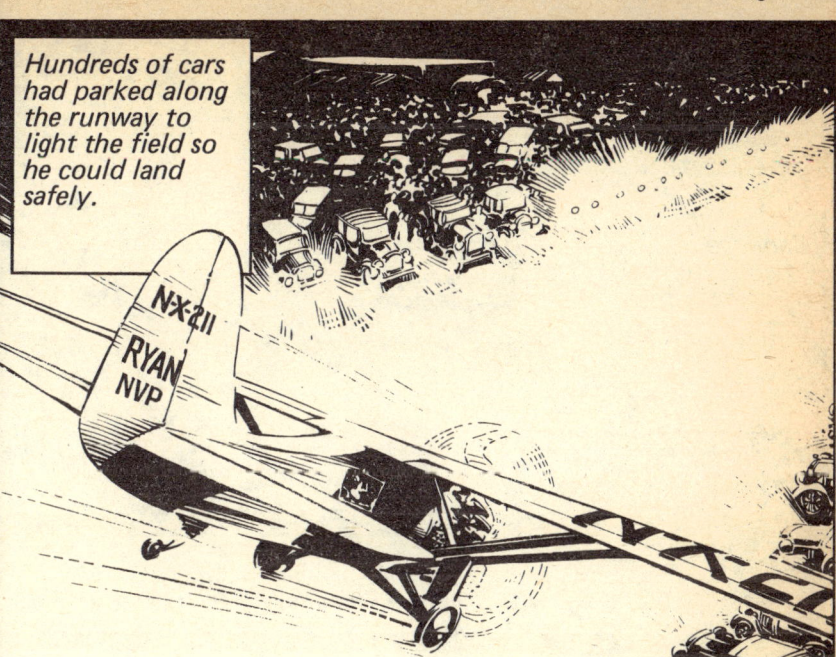

Charles Lindbergh 25

Hundreds of cars had parked along the runway to light the field so he could land safely.

He had flown from New York to Paris in thirty-three and one-half hours!

Charles Lindbergh was about to find out what it was like to be the most famous* man in the world.

*well known

*small, fast warships armed with guns
**huge airships that look like oval balloons

Charles Lindbergh 27

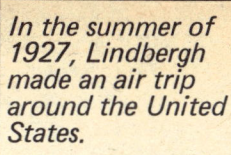

In the summer of 1927, Lindbergh made an air trip around the United States.

He flew 22,350 miles. He led parades in eighty-two cities and stayed at least one night in every state in the country. He wanted to prove that the air age had arrived.

That fall he made the first nonstop trip from Washington, D. C. to Mexico City.

In Mexico he stayed with U.S. Ambassador* Dwight Morrow and his family.

There he met their daughter Anne. A year and a half later, they were married.

I think you and my daughter will enjoy talking. You have many of the same interests.

*a person sent by the government of one country to live in another country to spread good will

*person who makes sure a plane stays on the right course
**taken and held for money

*not found in many places
**the outdoors—birds, trees, flowers, animals

Do you remember?

Charles Lindbergh's father was:

a. a representative to Congress from Minnesota.
b. an explorer.   c. a car salesman.

Charles drove his mother from Minnesota to California when he was:

a. fifteen years old.   b. twenty years old.
      c. six years old.

After Lindbergh left the Air Corps, he earned money as:

a. an airplane mechanic.   b. an air mail pilot.
c. a flying teacher.

The airplane Lindbergh used to fly the Atlantic was called:

a. *Spirit of St. Louis.*
b. *Tinkerbell.*   c. *Bluebird.*

Words to know

Can you use these words in sentences of your own?

pioneer	compass	ambassador
barnstorming	Eiffel Tower	navigator
Army Air Corps	famous	rare

True or false

1. Although Lindbergh is known for his skill as a pilot, he was also a very good farmer.

2. Lindbergh was not much of a mechanic.

3. On his New York to Paris trip, Lindbergh had all the equipment he needed to help him find his way.

4. The people of Paris were not very happy to see him.

5. Lindbergh spent his last few years teaching young pilots to fly.

Questions to think about and discuss

1. What do you think was Lindbergh's greatest concern as he began his New York to Paris flight? Why do you think so?

2. What was the name of Lindbergh's famous plane? Why did he choose that name?

3. What good points or qualities did Lindbergh have which made it possible for him to fly the Atlantic? Do you think pilots today have the same qualities? Why or why not?

4. How was Lindbergh's life as a boy and as a young man different from the kind of life you lead today?

5. What interests did Lindbergh and his wife Anne have in common? Do you think that this was unusual in the 1920s, 1930s, and 1940s?

Amelia Earhart

Written by
NAUNERLE C. FARR

Illustrated by
VICATAN

a
VINCENT FAGO
production

Contents

The adventurous young girl	35-39
Amelia's first flights	40-47
Across the Atlantic	48-55
Lost over the Pacific	56-59
Questions for review	60-63

Amelia Earhart

She was a brave woman who had the will to prove that women could equal men—in flying and in life itself.

She was Amelia Earhart, the first woman to fly over the Atlantic Ocean in an airplane. First she flew as a passenger, then alone in her own small, single-engine airplane.

Looks like there's a storm coming.

Yes, they have bad storms here.

Amelia Earhart was born in Atchison, Kansas, on July 24, 1898. Her grandparents had arrived years before in a covered wagon.

*a person who helps settle a new land

**someone who defends others in a court of law

… full, loose pants which were worn by women in the early 1900s
…a large fair held in 1904

Back in Atchison again, Amelia had an idea.
Let's build a roller coaster!
But—how can we?
We'll make a track by nailing these boards to the roof!
For a car I can put my roller skates on the bottom of this box.
We'll draw straws to see who goes first.
Oh, you go, Amelia.
You worked hardest

A happy Amelia climbed to the top of the slide. She sat down and gave a push.

Here I come! It's great!

At the end of the track the car hit the ground and stopped. Amelia flew through the air!

Oooooh!

Are you hurt, Amelia?

Of course not! I see what's wrong. The track must come out farther at the bottom. Let's fix it!

But Grandma put a stop to their plans.

That thing is dangerous! Why did you do such a thing, Amelia?

For fun, Grandma!

Amelia enjoyed reading adventure stories.

Reading is a nice way for a young lady to spend her time.

One thing makes me mad, though. The heroes are always boys or men!

Why shouldn't girls have adventures? Someday I will!

In 1908, when Amelia was ten years old, her father took the girls to the Iowa State Fair.

Please, Papa... one more ride?

I want to ride the *real* ponies!

Let's go to see the flying machine instead!

At last they reached the flying field.

The first aeroplane* flew only five years ago. Now you are seeing one!

But Amelia didn't think much of the airplane.

*airplane

Amelia Earhart 41

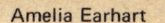

Several years passed. Muriel went to college in Toronto, Canada. In 1917, during World War I, Amelia went to visit her.

Oh, Muriel, until I came here I never knew what war meant!

It's not just soldiers and bands playing. It's men being hurt! I must stay and help!

The hospitals are full of wounded* men.

Amelia wrote to her mother.

Instead of returning to school, I want to become a nurses' aide.**

Her mother agreed to let her stay.

She worked at the Spadina Military Hospital for twelve hours every day.

She scrubbed floors.

She helped the wounded men.

Would you rub my back?

She carried trays.

Not rice pudding *again!*

For the rest of her life, Amelia would be strongly against war.

*hurt, injured
**someone who helps the nurses in a hospital

42 PENDULUM ILLUSTRATED BIOGRAPHY SERIES

Once, when she was not working, a friend took Amelia to the airfield where the Royal Air Corps* was trained.

So that's what flying can be! It's so beautiful.

Oh, Captain Spaulding, I want to fly!

I am really sorry, but there are rules against it.

I'm sorry, too. Someday I *will* fly!

When the war was over, Amelia went to New York and entered Columbia University. She would study to be a doctor. After a year she decided to leave school.

I'm sorry you are leaving. You would be a good doctor.

I just don't think this is my true work.

Amelia went to California. Her parents had moved there, and they wanted her to come and stay with them.

*the men who flew planes for Canada

Amelia Earhart 43

Soon after she arrived, her father took her to an air show. A surprised crowd watched as a man stood on the wing of a plane.

OOooooh!

Another plane flew by. The man reached for a rope hanging from it, missed, reached again, and grabbed it.

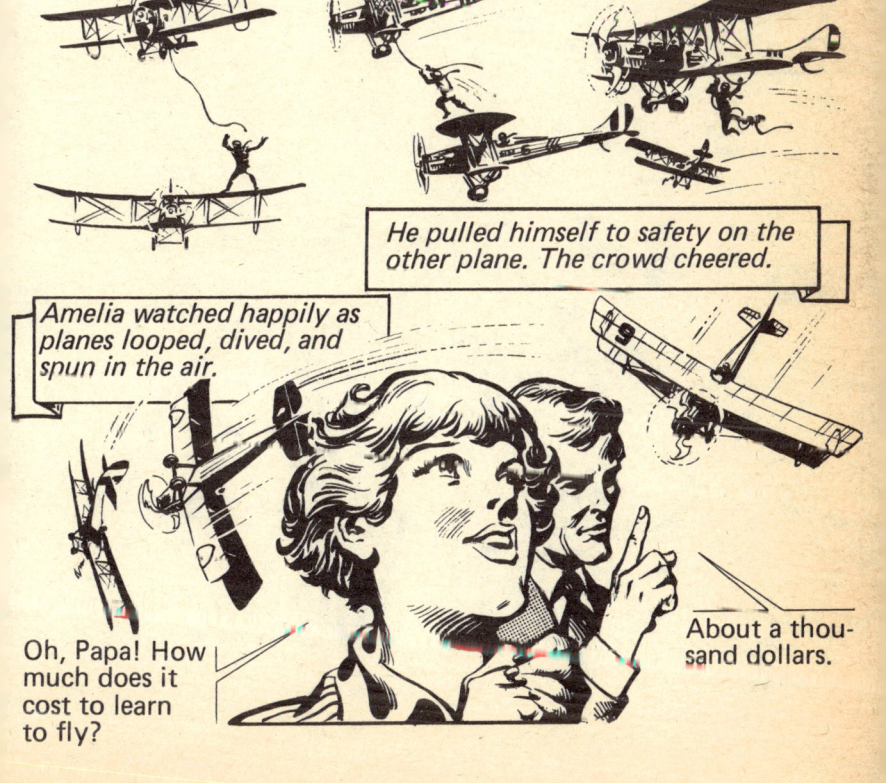

He pulled himself to safety on the other plane. The crowd cheered.

Amelia watched happily as planes looped, dived, and spun in the air.

Oh, Papa! How much does it cost to learn to fly?

About a thousand dollars.

A thousand dollars! May I at least go up for a ride?

If you are brave enough. I'll see to it.

The pilot for her first flight was Frank Hawks, winner of many speed records.

It's the best thing in the world!

Now she knew she had to fly. To pay for lessons she found a job with the telephone company.

Oh! Time to go to work!

Weekends were for flying. Amelia's teacher was Neta Snook, the first woman to finish at the Curtiss School of Aviation.*

Before you leave the ground, you must learn the parts of your plane.

*flying

Amelia Earhart 45

Slowly Amelia learned to fly, sometimes the hard way. Once her plane flipped over on landing.

"This looked like such a good, flat field!"

"There can always be a ditch that you can't see."

Later, Amelia took more lessons from John Montijo. He had taught Army pilots to fly.

"Stunts* are not just showing off, Amelia. They teach a pilot what to do when she's in trouble."

"I'm putting the plane into a spin. Take over and pull us out, Amelia!"

"Okay."

At last the great day came when she could fly alone. She took her plane down the field and into the air.

"She seems very calm."

"She's a good pilot. To her, the plane is like part of herself!"

*tricks

For her twenty-fourth birthday, on July 24, 1922, Amelia's parents and Muriel helped her buy a small yellow plane.

It's exactly what I wanted—light enough so I can pick up the tail and turn it around myself!

That October, she gave her parents tickets to an air show at Rogers Field.

That's my sister!

Ladies and gentlemen, Miss Amelia Earhart is about to try for a new women's altitude* record!

Amelia flew up and away until her little plane was only a speck in the sky.

She'll never make it in that small plane!

*height or distance above the ground

Amelia Earhart 47

Later, she landed safely as the crowd cheered.

The sealed barograph* from Miss Earhart's plane shows she reached 14,000 feet—a new women's record!

This was the first of many records Amelia would set.

A short time later, her parents decided to end their marriage.

"Mother wants to go back to Boston with us. How will we do it?"

"There's only one way. I'll have to sell my plane."

With the money she received, Amelia bought a car.

"Driving across the country is an adventure, too."

*In Boston Amelia had many different jobs. Finally she began working at a settlement house.***

"I want to see how high I can pile them before they fall!"

"You are trying to learn something, Ferris. That's good!"

*an instrument that measures air pressure and helps to show how high something is
*a place that provided services for people living in a city

One day in April, 1928, she and the children were preparing a play.
Telephone call for Miss Earhart!
Tell them to call back later. I'm busy.

But the caller said it was very important. Amelia went to the phone.
This is Captain Hilton Railey. Will you do something important to help aviation?
What do you want me to do?
I want you to fly across the Atlantic Ocean.
Of course! Who could turn down such an adventure?

The year before, young Charles Lindbergh had flown the Atlantic Ocean alone to become a world hero. Three women had died trying to do the same.
Mrs. Frederick Guest, an American, wanted a woman to make the flight. Captain Railey explained this to Amelia when she met him.
Mrs. Guest has bought an airplane. She wants it to fly from America to England with a woman on board.
Would I be the pilot?

Amelia Earhart 49

No. There will be a male pilot and a mechanic.*

I see.

If you are interested, you must go to New York. There they will choose the passenger.

I'll go at once!

Amelia was chosen to make the flight. She traveled to Boston to meet the pilot and see the plane.

This is Bill Stultz, the pilot, and Lou Gordan, the mechanic.

And this is the *Friendship!* They're fitting her with pontoons** for landing on water.

They had to wait several weeks for the right weather. George Palmer Putnam, one of the men in charge, spent his free time with Amelia.

How did you get into all this, Mr. Putnam?

Oh, I'm a friend of Lindbergh's. I guess I just like to be with people who have adventures!

*someone who fixes motors and engines
**objects like sled runners that are placed beneath an airplane to make it float

On June 3, they flew as far as Newfoundland.* They had to wait two weeks there. Then on June 17, 1928, they took off for England.

In another twenty-four hours they might be heroes. Or they might be dead.

Shortly after takeoff, they ran into a storm.

Amelia kept a record of what happened.

Bill says the radio is out.

They flew all day and into the night. Were they on the right course?**

Sure wish I could check where we are!

We'd better be getting *somewhere!*

One of the motors is stalling. I'll dive and try to start it up. Hold on, Amelia!

*an island in the Atlantic Ocean east of Canada
**route, planned direction

Amelia Earhart 51

At 3,000 feet they came out of the fog into dawn light. There was a ship below!

I'll tie a note to an orange and try to hit the ship! I'll ask them to point toward the nearest land!

She tried twice, using the last two oranges. Both missed!

We should see land by now. We have enough gas left for only one hour. Do we land near the ship—or go on?

They went on. Soon they saw small boats below.

Fishing boats! The coast must be near . . . but which way?

And then there it was—land ahead!

Is it England or Ireland?

Who cares? All I want is some calm water to land on!

> Bill made a good landing. Lou tied up the plane to keep it from floating away. Amelia waved to a man on shore.

We've crossed two thousand miles of ocean—in twenty hours and forty minutes!

Where is everybody?

> Soon a boat appeared.

We've just flown over from America. Where are we?

Welcome to Burry Port, Wales!*

> Soon they were welcomed on shore.

There's a great crowd of people waiting to see you, Miss.

Not me—I didn't do anything! It's Bill and Lou who did the flying.

> The news flashed around the world. For two weeks they were honored in England. Then they went home to a parade in New York City.

There's Lady Lindy!

Hurray for the first Lady of the Air!

Three cheers for Amelia!

> Everywhere it was the same. It was Amelia, the first woman to fly across the Atlantic, who was cheered by the crowds.

*an area in England

Amelia Earhart 53

But Amelia was unhappy. She talked with George Putnam who was now her friend and manager.

I have to fly the Atlantic by myself!

You will do it, I know!

But for now, you must write a book about the *Friendship* flight. We'll call it *Twenty Hours, Forty Minutes.*

Amelia finished the book in a few weeks. Then she returned to flying.

She had bought a small plane in England. She planned to fly across the United States in it.

I'll do it in short hops. I'll stop at night to sleep and to get fuel.

It will be the first time a woman has flown across the country and back again!

From the air, one small town looked like another to Amelia. There were no signs and few airports. One night when her gas was running low, she landed on the main street of Hobbs, New Mexico.

But she reached California and flew home again with no big problems.

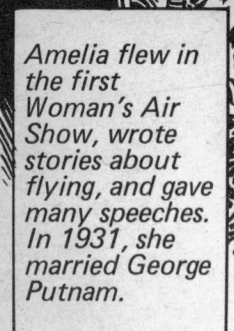

54 PENDULUM ILLUSTRATED BIOGRAPHY SERIES

It was an unusual* marriage.

Amelia flew in the first Woman's Air Show, wrote stories about flying, and gave many speeches. In 1931, she married George Putnam.

I must be free to do my work and to fly. And you must promise to let me go in a year if we are not happy.

I promise!

Amelia kept working to improve her flying. She never forgot her desire to fly across the Atlantic alone. At last, about 7:00 PM on May 20, 1932, she took off from Newfoundland in her airplane.

She climbed to 10,000 feet. The weather was good.

Then something went wrong.

The altimeter** is out! I can't tell how high I am!

All at once the plane was in heavy storm clouds.

I'll try to climb above the clouds. But if I go too high, the plane will ice up!

*something new or different
**an instrument that measures how high a plane is

> Soon, ice began forming on the wings. The plane went into a spin.

> It fell 3,000 feet. The ice melted in the warmer air, and Amelia pulled out of the spin.

That water was too close for comfort!

> Suddenly, flames shot out of a crack in the plane's tailpipes. She flew on, hoping it would hold together. Dawn came. She saw land ahead. There were mountains and a railroad.

Perhaps the railroad will lead me to a city with an airport.

> Instead, she found a meadow where she made a smooth landing. She had flown from America to Londonderry, Ireland, in fifteen hours, eighteen minutes.

Hello! I've come from America!

Have you, now?

> At last she had flown a plane across the Atlantic, alone... the first woman to do it!

In London, the king sent his praise, and she danced with the Prince of Wales.

In Paris they gave her a medal.

The Cross of the Legion of Honor.*

The king of Belgium gave her another medal.

Allow my country to honor you.

Back in America she was called to the White House. And President Hoover gave her still another medal.

You are a true American pioneer!

Thank you, Mr. President. I am honored!

Then Amelia flew over the Pacific Ocean from Hawaii to California, the first person, man or woman, to make the flight. Finally, she landed in Newark, New Jersey.

At the airport she and her plane were cheered wildly by the crowds.

*a medal given to someone for actions or deeds that deserve praise

Amelia Earhart 57

In 1935, Amelia went to teach at a college in Indiana. She often talked with the women students.

If there is a job you want to try—do it! Don't let being a woman stop you from trying any job!

The college raised money for a special Amelia Earhart Fund.

We have $50,000 to buy you a new airplane!

The Electra was the largest, safest plane she had ever owned. She talked to George about her new plan.

I want to fly around the world in it—at the equator.* That's the route no one has flown before.

If that's what you want, I'll do all I can to help you.

While Amelia studied flight charts, George arranged to have gasoline and spare parts at the faraway places where she would need them.

*In March, she and Fred Noonan, her navigator,** flew to Hawaii. On her next takeoff, something went wrong. There was a crash.*

Are you all right?

Yes, and I'll try again!

*an imaginary line around the center of the earth
**someone who sets the course of a plane or ship

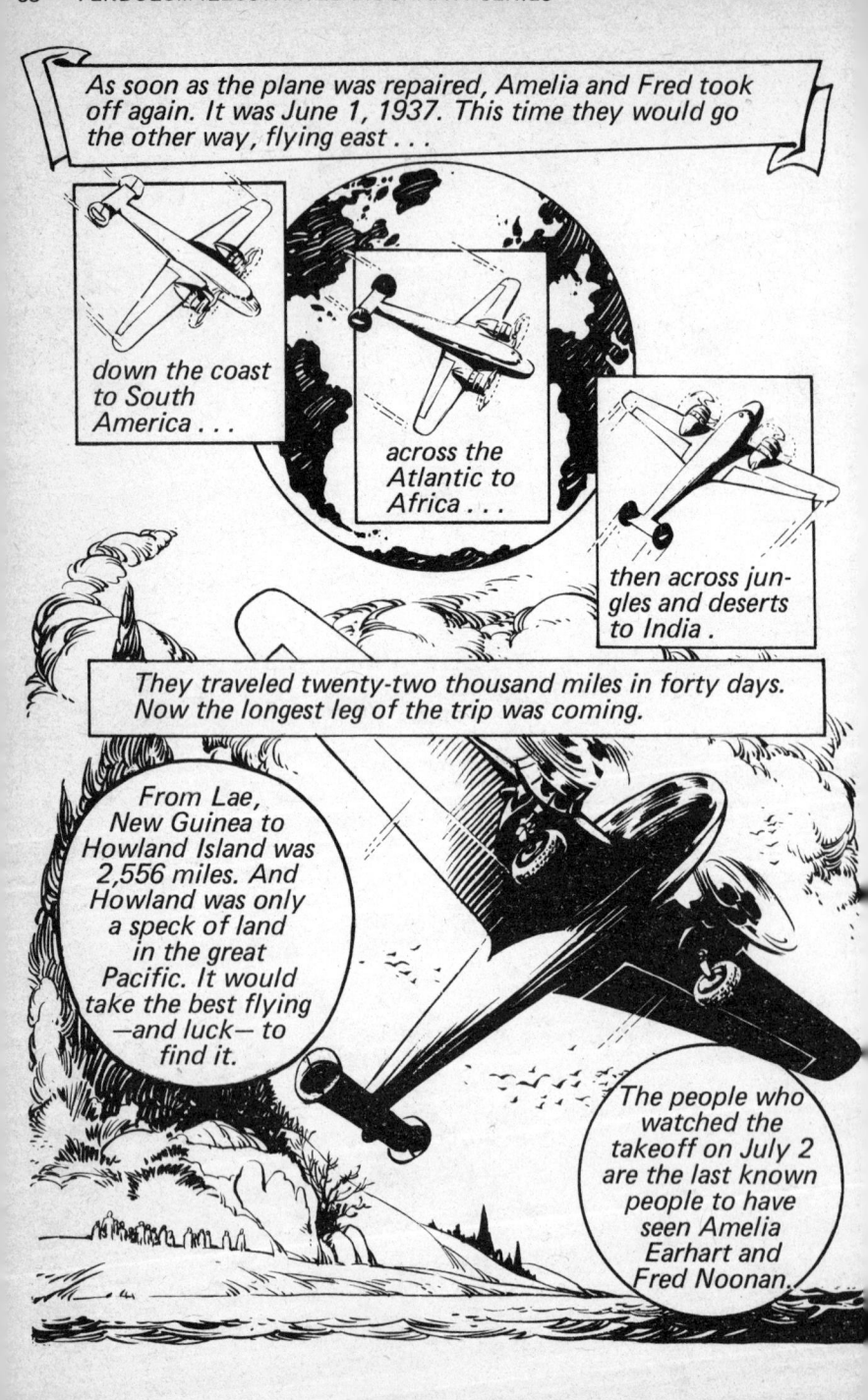

As soon as the plane was repaired, Amelia and Fred took off again. It was June 1, 1937. This time they would go the other way, flying east...

down the coast to South America...

across the Atlantic to Africa...

then across jungles and deserts to India.

They traveled twenty-two thousand miles in forty days. Now the longest leg of the trip was coming.

From Lae, New Guinea to Howland Island was 2,556 miles. And Howland was only a speck of land in the great Pacific. It would take the best flying —and luck— to find it.

The people who watched the takeoff on July 2 are the last known people to have seen Amelia Earhart and Fred Noonan.

Amelia Earhart 59

The Coast Guard boat Itaska was supposed to help guide Amelia. All night it signaled to her.

But Amelia's radio was not receiving the Itaska's signals. Daylight came, and then there was a final message.

Itaska from Earhart... we're about 100 miles out... please take a bearing* on us and report...

Earhart from Itaska... we are sending signals... please come in...

Cannot see you. Gas is running low. Can't reach you by radio...

At ten o'clock, when her plane would have run out of gas, the United States Navy started the largest sea search in history.

Five ships and sixty planes searched for Amelia's plane. No trace of the Electra or its passengers was found.

It was hard to believe that Amelia Earhart was dead.

Yet how she died is not important. The thirty-nine years of Amelia Earhart's life proved how much one woman could do.

THE END

*send signals to a plane to show exactly where it is

Do you remember?

Amelia entered college to study:

a. nursing.   b. medicine.   c. teaching.

To pay for her flying lessons, Amelia had to get up early and get to her job with:

a. the telephone company.   b. the railroad.
c. the pizza shop.

Amelia Earhart 61

Because she was the first woman to fly across the Atlantic, the crowds cheered Amelia as:

a. Miss Friendship.
b. Wonder Woman.
c. Lady Lindy.

When she was seen for the last time, Amelia was:

a. trying to fly around the world.
b. flying from coast to coast.
c. flying to the moon.

Words to know

Can you use these words in sentences of your own?

equator	settlement house	aviation
altimeter	bloomers	pontoons
navigator	pioneer	stunts

True or false

1. Amelia's family gave her all the money she needed for flying lessons.

2. Amelia was the first woman who had tried to cross the Atlantic in a plane.

3. The first time Amelia saw an airplane, she knew right away that she wanted to fly.

4. Amelia always felt that women could do most of the things men could do—if they were only given the chance.

5. Amelia crashed several times in her planes. This made her a bit afraid of flying again.

Questions to think about and discuss

1. What were some of the dangers of flying in Amelia's time? Are the dangers the same or different today?

2. What medals and honors did Amelia receive for her flying adventures?

3. How did it happen that Amelia's last plane was lost at sea? What do you think finally happened to her? Why?

4. In what way was Amelia "a true American pioneer" as President Hoover called her?

5. What fields of work are opening to women today that will give them a chance to be like Amelia?